The MAILBOX®
The Education Center

Read-Aloud Roundup

grades K-1

A bonanza of learning activities based on 50 favorite books!

- ⭐ **Literacy activities**
- ⭐ **Math activities**
- ⭐ **Science activities**
- ⭐ **Social studies activities**
- ⭐ **Writing prompts**
- ⭐ **Discussion questions**
- ⭐ **Practice pages**
- ⭐ **Patterns**

Managing Editors: Tina Petersen and Kelly Robertson

Editorial Team: Becky S. Andrews, Diane Badden, Kimberley Bruck, Karen A. Brudnak, Pam Crane, Chris Curry, Laura Del Prete, Amy Erickson, Pierce Foster, Laurie K. Gibbons, Tazmen Hansen, Marsha Heim, Lori Z. Henry, Laura Johnson, Debra Liverman, Kitty Lowrance, Gerri Primak, Mark Rainey, Greg D. Rieves, Hope Rodgers, Rebecca Saunders, Leanne S. Swinson, Donna K. Teal, Rachael Traylor, Sharon M. Tresino, Susan Walker, Zane Williard, Barbara Mason Worobey

www.themailbox.com

Printed in the United States
10 9 8 7 6 5 4 3 2 1

HPS 227020

Table of Contents

What's Inside

50 featured read-alouds!

100 activities!

164 discussion questions!

50 writing prompts!

25 patterns and reproducibles!

All of this in an easy-to-read format!

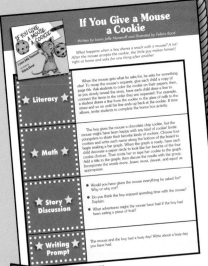

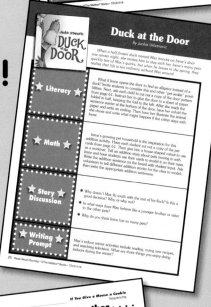

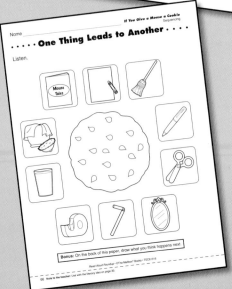

Alexander and the Terrible, Horrible, No Good, Very Bad Day

Written by Judith Viorst and illustrated by Ray Cruz

Alexander is having a very bad day. He wakes up with gum in his hair, his best friend chooses a new best friend, he gets in trouble for fighting, and there's kissing on TV!

★ Literacy ★

If only some things had happened differently, perhaps Alexander's day wouldn't have been so bad! First, ask students to recall some of the bad things that happen to Alexander. List these events on the board. Then ask each child to pick an event from the list and rewrite the event so it becomes a positive moment for Alexander. After each child illustrates his work, bind the completed pages into a class book titled "Alexander and the Very Good Day!"

★ Social Studies ★

When bad things happen to Alexander, he's certain he needs to move to Australia. On a world map, show students their current location and the country of Australia. Remind students that koalas and kangaroos live in Australia. Also use the map to show students that Australia is surrounded by water, which means it has lots of beaches. Then ask each child to illustrate the kind of day Alexander thinks he could have there.

★ Story Discussion ★

- Why do you think Alexander wants to move to Australia? Does this seem like a good solution to a bad day? Why or why not?

- Which event in the story reminds you of something that has happened to you? Explain.

- In your opinion, what is the worst thing that happens to Alexander? Explain.

- How could Alexander improve his day?

★ Writing Prompt ★

Alexander's mother is right—everyone has a bad day every once in a while. Write five tips for turning a bad day into a good day.

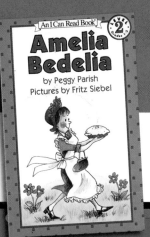

Amelia Bedelia

Written by Peggy Parish and illustrated by Fritz Siebel

When Amelia Bedelia begins working for Mrs. Rogers, her literal interpretation of instructions has hilarious results!

Literacy

What Mrs. Rogers wants Amelia Bedelia to do is quite different from what the befuddled housekeeper does! Revisit Mrs. Rogers' instructions with students and discuss the words that might be confusing to the housekeeper. Next, ask each student to visually divide a sheet of paper in half. Have him title one half "Mrs. Rogers" and the other half "Amelia Bedelia." Then instruct him to illustrate below the appropriate headings how Mrs. Rogers expects a chore to be done and how Amelia Bedelia actually completes it.

Math

Amelia Bedelia's misuse of a measuring tape is a perfect springboard for a review of measurement tools. Reread to students the pages that tell about Amelia Bedelia measuring rice. After students describe how the housekeeper should complete the task, draw a T chart on the board. Label one column with an illustration of a measuring cup and the other column with an illustration of a measuring tape. Have students name things that are typically measured with each tool; then write the items in the appropriate columns.

Story Discussion

- If you were Mr. or Mrs. Rogers, would you fire Amelia Bedelia after seeing all her housekeeping mistakes? Why or why not?

- Which of Amelia Bedelia's mistakes do you think is the funniest? Why?

- Do you think Amelia Bedelia is well suited for doing household chores? Explain.

Writing Prompt

Write a note to Amelia Bedelia giving instructions for cleaning your room. Be sure to explain exactly what she needs to do.

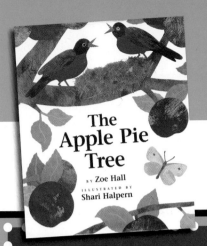

The Apple Pie Tree

Written by Zoe Hall and illustrated by Shari Halpern

Two sisters delight in observing the seasonal changes of a cherished apple tree.

 **Literacy**

How does the tree transform during the year? That's what your students recap with this skill-boosting idea! Revisit several tree illustrations in sequential order and prompt students to recall corresponding story details. Next, give each youngster a copy of page 55. Have her cut out the tree illustrations and glue them where indicated to reflect the order of the story events. Then ask her to label each illustration with the corresponding season.

Science

This booklet activity reminds students that they grow and change just as the tree and robins do. For each student, stack two vertical sheets of paper. Slide the top paper upward about one inch. Fold the papers forward to create graduated pages and then staple along the fold. Have each child title his booklet "Changes." Ask him to label the bottom edge of the first page "Baby," the next page "Child," and the last page "Adult." After he illustrates the first two pages with corresponding self-portraits, instruct him to draw on the last page what he imagines he will look like as an adult.

 **Story Discussion**

- The children in the story watch the tree grow every year. What changes do you think will happen next?

- During which season do you think the girls enjoy the tree the most? Why?

- Which do you think would be more fun to watch as it changes: an apple tree or a baby robin? Explain.

 **Writing Prompt**

The girls wait a long time for the tree to grow apples. Think of a time you waited for something. What did you wait for and how long did you wait?

Arthur's Eyes
By Marc Brown

Arthur the aardvark learns, with his teacher's help, that wearing glasses isn't so bad after all!

★ Literacy ★

A new pair of glasses seems to be the perfect solution to Arthur's eyesight problems—until his new glasses become a problem too! Have volunteers describe how Arthur tries to solve this latest problem and explain why each solution doesn't work. Also ask students how Mr. Marco (Arthur's teacher) helps Arthur tackle the problem he's having. To recap, write on chart paper the title "When You Can't Solve a Problem, Look for Help." Post the title and surround it with student-drawn self-portraits to which each child has attached a pair of stylish paper spectacles!

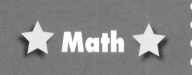

★ Math ★

Arthur is self-conscious about wearing his spectacles because he doesn't see anyone else wearing glasses. For a quick review of tally marks, draw a T chart on the board. Label one column "yes" and one column "no." Ask the question "Does anyone in your family wear glasses?" Invite each child, in turn, to draw a tally mark on the chart to record his response. Afterward, have students compare the results using words such as *more, fewer,* and *equal* as appropriate. Repeat the activity with additional yes-or-no questions, such as "Have you ever worn 3-D glasses?" and "Do you like to wear sunglasses?"

★ Story Discussion ★

- What problems does Arthur have before he gets glasses?
- Were you surprised when Arthur's friends teased him? Why?
- How do Arthur's feelings about wearing his glasses change during the story?
- Why do you think Francine wears her movie star glasses at the end of the story?

★ Writing Prompt ★

Write two or more things that Arthur's experience with new glasses taught you.

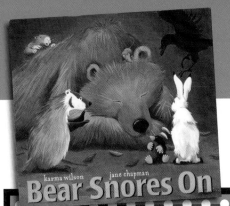

Bear Snores On

Written by Karma Wilson and illustrated by Jane Chapman

While Bear naps, forest animals take shelter in his cave and have an impromptu party. Their gathering eventually wakes Bear, but instead of asking his uninvited guests to leave, he wants to be included in the fun!

Literacy

The vivid description of each animal's entrance into the cave begs to be acted out! Revisit the pages where the animals enter the cave and discuss with students the meanings of any unfamiliar words. Then assign the role of each cave visitor to a different student. Ask the other students to share the bear's role. As you reread the story, have each actor pantomime his assigned animal's actions. It's a surefire way to bring the story and vocabulary to life!

Literacy

What better way to follow up this rhyme-filled tale than with rhyming practice! Use cardboard tubes (logs) and flame cutouts to make a mock campfire. Sit with students around the fire and dim the lights. Then name a word. Have the student beside you say a rhyming word. Then continue around the circle with each youngster naming a different rhyming word. When students can't come up with any more rhyming words, name a different word for them to rhyme with. There's no doubt students will be eager to see how far around the circle they can go!

Story Discussion

- What details let you know the story could not really happen?
- Do you ever wake up grumpy like Bear? Explain.
- What do you do when you have trouble falling asleep?

Writing Prompt

What three things would you take to the party in Bear's cave? Why?

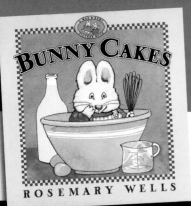

Bunny Cakes

By Rosemary Wells

Max makes an earthworm cake for Grandma's birthday and then eagerly tries to help his big sister, Ruby, with her cake preparations.

Literacy

The bunnies' birthday preparations do not go smoothly! Remind students that both Ruby and her little brother Max have problems in the story. To identify Ruby's main problem, ask students, "What is Ruby trying to do?" Then ask, "What problem is Ruby having?" and "How does Ruby solve her problem?" In a similar manner, help students discover a problem that Max is able to solve (*getting some Red-Hot Marshmallow Squirters*).

Math

Max and Ruby have ideas about how to decorate a special cake. No doubt your students have cake-decorating ideas too! Give each child a copy of page 56. A student uses the symbols in the code to decorate the cake. Each time she adds a decoration to the cake, she colors the matching amount of money. Encourage her to spend her entire cake-decorating budget!

Story Discussion

● Does Max break the eggs and spill the milk and flour on purpose? Explain.

● Why does Ruby write a list for Max each time he goes to the grocery store?

● Do you think Grandma likes her cakes? Explain.

● Can Max read? Can Max write? How do you know?

Writing Prompt

Pretend you are going to the grocery store. Make a list of the items you would like to buy.

See page 57 for a reproducible activity.

Chicka Chicka Boom Boom

Written by Bill Martin Jr. and John Archambault and illustrated by Lois Ehlert

All the lowercase letters playfully race to the top of a coconut tree. Once they're at the top, the tree flops, the letters drop, and the uppercase letters rush to the rescue!

★ Literacy ★

Who can resist the challenge of racing to the top of a coconut tree? Certainly not your students! Display a large tree cutout within student reach on a magnetic surface. Give each youngster a magnetic letter. As you read the story, have each youngster put his letter at the top of the tree the first time you name it. After you read the page on which the letters fall, push the magnetic letters to the base of the tree. Then continue reading, pausing for each student to put his letter back on the tree when he hears it named again.

★ Literacy ★

When the lowercase letters take a nasty tumble, the uppercase letters rush to their sides. Invite students to show how the letters pair up with this kid-pleasing activity. Display lowercase letter cards in a pocket chart. Give each youngster a corresponding uppercase letter card. Then say, "Skit skat skoodle doot. Flip flop flee. Watch [Kara, Johnny, and Darius] pair the letters for me!" Have the named students put their cards with the matching lowercase letter cards. Continue the activity until all the letters are correctly paired.

★ Story Discussion ★

- Why do you think the letters fall?

- Describe a time you fell or got hurt and an adult helped you.

- At the end of the story, the letter A says, "Dare double dare..." What does *dare* mean? Is it good to take a dare?

★ Writing Prompt ★

Would you like to climb a real coconut tree? Why or why not?

Chrysanthemum
By Kevin Henkes

Chrysanthemum adores her name. In fact, she thinks it's absolutely perfect—until her first day of school.

Literacy

Remind students that Chrysanthemum loves the way her name looks when it is written. Set out an assortment of writing utensils, including markers, crayons, and colored pencils. Invite each child to write her own name several times on a blank sheet of paper using a variety of supplies and different writing styles.

Science

Victoria can't get over the fact that Chrysanthemum is named for a flower. If possible, provide a chrysanthemum and a delphinium (commonly known as larkspur) flower for students to investigate. If flowers are not available, provide pictures or photos. Ask students why a parent might choose one of these names for a child. Then give each youngster a copy of page 58 to complete. Finally, encourage students to tell how the two flowers are alike.

Story Discussion

- Who is the better friend, Victoria or Chrysanthemum? Explain.

- What is the most important thing about a person's name? Explain.

- If you could change your name, would you? Why or why not?

Writing Prompt

In the end, Chrysanthemum knows her name is perfect for her. What are some things you like about your name?

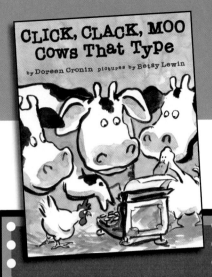

Click, Clack, Moo: Cows That Type

Written by Doreen Cronin and illustrated by Betsy Lewin

A herd of clever dairy cows uses its amazing typing and negotiating skills to get electric blankets delivered to the barn.

The cows and hens ask for electric blankets, and the ducks demand a diving board. Ask students, "What do you think other farm animals might want from Farmer Brown?" To answer, have each child draw a farm animal and an item it might request. Encourage students to write captions for their drawings.

For an engaging word study, return to selected pages in the book and read aloud the onomatopoeic words, such as *click, clack, moo,* and *quack*. Explain that these words sound just like the noises they describe. Draw the outline of a barn on the board. Then write around the barn an assortment of onomatopoeic words that describe the sounds a farmer might hear, such as *oink, meow, splat, crunch, bang, chirp,* and *neigh*.

- What details prove this story could not really happen?

- What does the cows' experience teach you about making demands?

- Do you think Farmer Brown asks the ducks to do anything before he gives them a diving board? Why or why not?

- What other old items might the cows find in the barn? What might they do with these items?

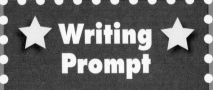

Write a letter to Farmer Brown. Tell him why you would like to visit his farm.

Cloudy With a Chance of Meatballs

Written by Judi Barrett and illustrated by Ron Barrett

Grandpa tells a tall tale featuring Chewandswallow, an unusual town where the daily weather report also is the menu. It's a great place to live until the weather takes a turn for the worse!

Literacy

Whether a resident of Chewandswallow likes the weather depends on his food preferences. What forecasts would tantalize your students' taste buds? To find out, give each youngster a sheet of paper. Have him label the front "Good Weather" and the back "Bad Weather." Ask him to illustrate an appropriate forecast for Chewandswallow on each side of the paper and then write captions for his work. Don't be surprised if you see downpours of chocolate ice cream!

Literacy

Grandpa's pancake mishap inspires him to tell the story of Chewandswallow. Encourage students to imagine how Grandpa's story would be different if he loses control of a toy, such as modeling clay, instead of a pancake. Then have the class make a toy-themed mural that shows what the weather might be like in a town named Shareandplay. Write a class paragraph about the playful town and display it with the mural.

Story Discussion

● What would be good about living in a town where food comes from the sky? What would not be good about it?

● Do you think the day's temperature affects what foods are in the Chewandswallow forecast? Explain.

● What do you think the townspeople would see if they ever returned to Chewandswallow?

Writing Prompt

Write a morning forecast for Chewandswallow. Use words that tell how the food-themed weather looks, smells, tastes, and feels.

Corduroy
By Don Freeman

A department-store teddy bear realizes that a button missing from his overalls might jeopardize his chance of being purchased. After he searches for the button in vain, he happily discovers that his new friend likes him just the way he is.

★ Literacy ★

Corduroy learns that a pair of overalls isn't the only thing that has buttons—mattresses have buttons too! For this phonological awareness activity, instruct each youngster to position a large unlined index card (mattress) horizontally. As you say a word from the story, have each student put on the mattress one round counter (button) per syllable. Then ask her to repeat the word as she touches each button, in turn. After you confirm the number of syllables, have youngsters clear their mattresses to prepare for a different word.

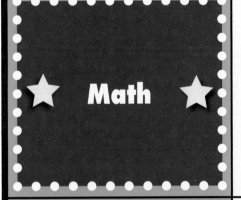
★ Math ★

One less button makes a big difference for Corduroy! To explore the concept of one less, have each child put a designated number of counters (buttons) on an overalls cutout (pattern on page 59). Then ask how many buttons would be left if one button were lost. Have him model and solve the problem. After he solves similar problems, instruct him to attach the following cutouts to the overalls: a bear head, a neck, two arms, and two feet. Then invite him to complete the outfit with button illustrations.

★ Story Discussion ★

- Why do you think Lisa doesn't want a box for Corduroy after she purchases him?

- What makes Lisa happy? What makes Corduroy happy?

- In the end, Corduroy discovers what a friend is. How would you explain what a friend is?

★ Writing Prompt ★

Write about something you or someone you know lost.

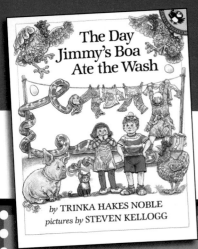

by TRINKA HAKES NOBLE
pictures by STEVEN KELLOGG

The Day Jimmy's Boa Ate the Wash

Written by Trinka Hakes Noble and illustrated by Steven Kellogg

When Jimmy's unusual pet accompanies him on a class trip, an ordinary day at the farm turns into a hysterical disaster!

★ Literacy ★

This engaging recap of a field trip gone wrong is packed with vivid examples of cause and effect. During a second reading of the story, have students identify the cause of each of several incidents, such as why the haystack falls over, why the students start throwing eggs, and why the pigs eat the students' lunches. For a fun follow-up, have each child fold a sheet of paper in half and then unfold it. Ask each student to label the right half of his paper "Effect" and illustrate a real or made-up story event in the corresponding space. Then have him label the left half of his paper "Cause" and illustrate what causes the event to happen.

★ Literacy ★

Does a boa constrictor eat laundry? Does a pig eat corn? Can a chicken lay an egg on your head? Challenge students to sort facts from fiction. Give each child a large T-shirt cutout on which to illustrate something from the story that really could happen. Display the illustrated clothing on a mock clothesline with the title "This Much Is True!"

★ Story Discussion ★

● Who is telling this story? How do you know?

● Do you think Jimmy will tell his parents about the field trip? Why?

● Why do you think Jimmy takes his boa to the farm?

● Do you think Jimmy wants his boa constrictor back? Why or why not?

★ Writing Prompt ★

Write a list of rules that Mrs. Stanley's class should follow the next time they go on a field trip.

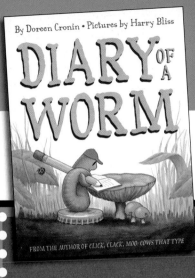

By Doreen Cronin • Pictures by Harry Bliss

DIARY OF A WORM

FROM THE AUTHOR OF *CLICK, CLACK, MOO-COWS THAT TYPE*

Diary of a Worm

Written by Doreen Cronin and illustrated by Harry Bliss

The daily activities of a complex and lovable worm are humorously captured in this one-of-a-kind diary.

★ Literacy ★

Is this diary-keeping worm all that different from a child? Most likely, students will laugh at the comparison, but they'll be curious too! Engage the class in retelling the tale from the point of view of a child. To begin, read the entry for March 20 and ask students whether they think there are three things a human mom wants her child to always remember. For the next entry ask, "Have you ever tried to teach a friend how to do something he's never done before? How well did it go?" Continue the retelling. By the end of the story, students will be ready to draw their own conclusions about the similarities between the diary keeper and themselves!

★ Science ★

By the end of this delightful story, students will be chuckling over and cheering for worms! Reread the story, this time asking students to listen carefully for factual information about worms. Ask students to share the facts they learn and help them investigate information about which they are uncertain. Lead students to conclude that worms have an important place in our environment.

★ Story ★ Discussion

- What is the purpose of a diary? Would you like to keep a diary? Why or why not?

- Why do you think the author uses a diary format to tell the story?

- Do you think the author has a sense of humor? Explain.

★ Writing ★ Prompt

Write a diary entry that describes something you did yesterday. Try to weave some humor into your entry.

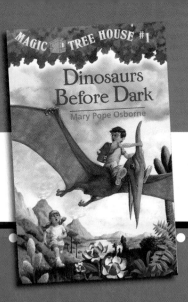

Dinosaurs Before Dark

By Mary Pope Osborne

Jack and his sister Annie find a mysterious tree house that whisks them away to prehistoric times. After escaping a few close calls with dinosaurs, they make it home before anyone knows they were gone.

Literacy

Visualizing Jack and Annie's incredible adventure is the next best thing to experiencing it! Give each youngster a blank ten-page booklet. Have him number the pages from one to ten. As you read the first chapter, instruct him to sketch on the first booklet page what he pictures in his mind. Then invite youngsters to tell the group about the details represented in their drawings. Repeat the drawing and sharing process with each remaining chapter. It's a picture-perfect way to boost comprehension and help youngsters remember story details.

Literacy

A lot happens to Jack and Annie in seemingly no time at all. Have students recap the amazing story events with this summary idea. Draw on a large piece of paper a simple tree house with a ten-rung ladder. Display the poster in a prominent classroom location. After students are familiar with the first chapter, write a student-generated one-sentence summary on the lowest blank rung. Continue with the remaining chapters to the top of the ladder!

Story Discussion

- When Annie wants Jack to feel the Pteranodon, she tells him, "Don't think...Just do it." Do you think that's good advice? Explain.

- Would you like to go on an adventure with Jack and Annie? Why or why not?

- Jack and Annie plan to return to the tree house and are eager to see what happens next. What do you think will happen next?

Writing Prompt

Annie is impulsive, while Jack is more thoughtful. Which character is more like you? Explain.

The Doorbell Rang

By Pat Hutchins

Ma makes a dozen delicious cookies, which should be plenty for her two children. However, the doorbell rings again and again, with more friends showing up each time.

Literacy

The children in this story are more than willing to share with their friends. Ask students to give examples of how they share with others. Possible examples include sharing toys, school supplies, snacks, hugs, and time. Invite students to describe times when they didn't want to share. Also find out how they feel when others do not share with them. Then have students make the booklet on page 60 as a reminder that sharing is the right thing to do!

Math

Each time more children arrive, Sam and Victoria divide the freshly baked cookies again. For a hands-on introduction to division, ask each child to draw a large rectangle (table) on her paper and draw two Xs at the table—one for Sam and one for Victoria. Next, have each child evenly divide 12 brown paper hole punches (cookies) between the Xs. Then reread the story, pausing each time the doorbell rings so students can add the new guests to their tables and redistribute the cookies.

Story Discussion

- On which day of the week do you think this story takes place? Why?

- Why does Ma keep saying "No one makes cookies like Grandma"?

- When the doorbell rings near the end of the story, why does Ma suggest that the children eat their cookies before she opens the door?

- Who do you think rings the doorbell at the very end of the story?

Writing Prompt

Draw the ingredients needed for your favorite kind of cookie. Then write directions for making and baking the cookies.

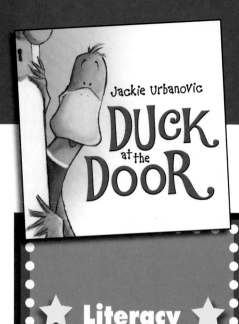

Duck at the Door
By Jackie Urbanovic

When a half-frozen duck named Max knocks on Irene's door one winter night, she invites him to stay with her. Irene's many pets quickly tire of Max's quirks, but when he leaves in the spring, they realize that life is too ordinary without Max around.

★ **Literacy** ★

What if Irene opens the door to find an alligator instead of a duck? Invite students to consider this and other "pet-acular" possibilities. Next, ask each child to cut out a copy of the door pattern from page 61. Instruct her to glue the door to a sheet of paper folded in half, keeping the fold to the left. After she reads the sentence starter at the bottom of the door, have her unfold the paper and write an ending. Then have her illustrate the animal she chose and write what might happen if the critter stays with Irene.

★ **Math** ★

Irene's growing pet household is the inspiration for this addition activity. Have each student cut out a copy of the pet cards from page 61. Then give him a house-shaped cutout to use as a workmat. Tell an addition story about pets moving in with Irene and have students use their cards to model it on their mats. Write the addition sentence on the board with student input. Ask volunteers to tell different addition stories for the class to model; then write the appropriate addition sentences.

★ **Story Discussion** ★

- Why doesn't Max fly south with the rest of his flock? Is this a good decision? Why or why not?

- In what ways does Max behave like a younger brother or sister to the other pets?

- Why do you think Irene has so many pets?

★ **Writing Prompt** ★

Max's indoor winter activities include reading, trying new recipes, and watching television. What are three things you enjoy doing indoors during the winter?

Elmer
By David McKee

Elmer is a brightly colored patchwork elephant who thinks he's tired of being different from all the other elephants—until he discovers that being unique is wonderful!

Literacy

Elmer is loved by his fellow elephants because he is fun to be around. To make a character web of Elmer's positive traits, have each child draw a large circle in the center of a blank sheet of paper and an oval in each corner. Then have him draw Elmer inside the circle. Next, write a list of positive traits on the board and ask students to decide which ones best describe Elmer. Traits might include playful, kind, happy, friendly, colorful, and funny. Have each child refer to the list to complete his web. Invite each child to make a second web about himself on the back of his paper!

Math

The other elephants are so tickled with Elmer's gray disguise that they decide once a year, on Elmer's Day, Elmer will wear his gray disguise and they will decorate themselves in his honor! Give each child a copy of page 62. Have him color one elephant gray. Then have him decorate one elephant with hearts, one with polka dots, one with stripes, one with a checkerboard pattern, and one with flowers. Next, have him cut out the cards and glue them in random order to a 4" x 18" paper strip. Engage students in using ordinal numbers to describe the locations of specific elephants in their "elephant parades."

Story Discussion

- Do you think the jungle animals, including the elephants in the herd, care that Elmer looks different? Explain.

- Do you think Elmer plays mean jokes on his elephant buddies? Why or why not?

- What does Elmer learn about being unique?

Writing Prompt

Elmer's patchwork coloring makes him unique. Describe ways in which you are unique.

Fish Eyes: A Book You Can Count On

By Lois Ehlert

A math-minded guppy leads the way through this visually striking underwater adventure.

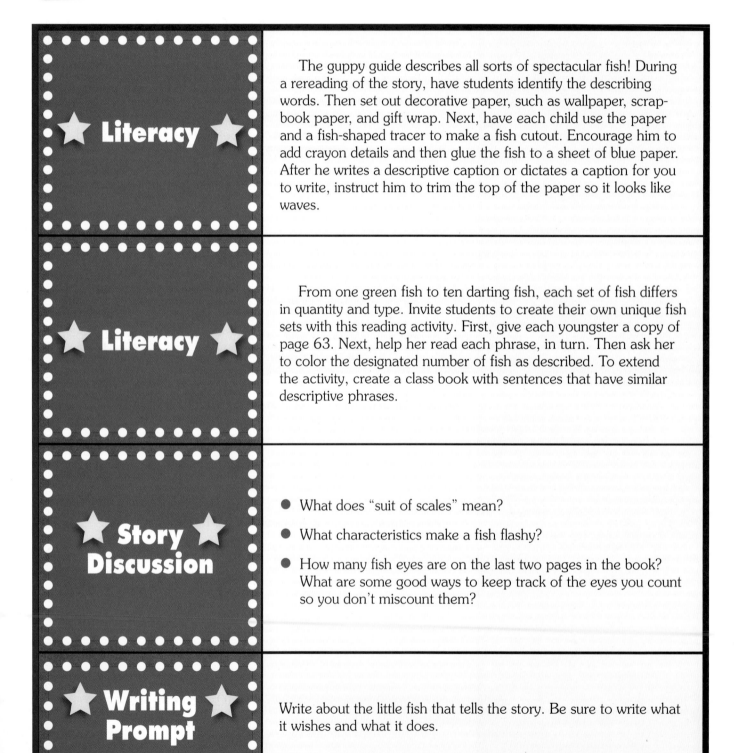

★ Literacy ★

The guppy guide describes all sorts of spectacular fish! During a rereading of the story, have students identify the describing words. Then set out decorative paper, such as wallpaper, scrapbook paper, and gift wrap. Next, have each child use the paper and a fish-shaped tracer to make a fish cutout. Encourage him to add crayon details and then glue the fish to a sheet of blue paper. After he writes a descriptive caption or dictates a caption for you to write, instruct him to trim the top of the paper so it looks like waves.

★ Literacy ★

From one green fish to ten darting fish, each set of fish differs in quantity and type. Invite students to create their own unique fish sets with this reading activity. First, give each youngster a copy of page 63. Next, help her read each phrase, in turn. Then ask her to color the designated number of fish as described. To extend the activity, create a class book with sentences that have similar descriptive phrases.

★ Story Discussion ★

- What does "suit of scales" mean?

- What characteristics make a fish flashy?

- How many fish eyes are on the last two pages in the book? What are some good ways to keep track of the eyes you count so you don't miscount them?

★ Writing Prompt ★

Write about the little fish that tells the story. Be sure to write what it wishes and what it does.

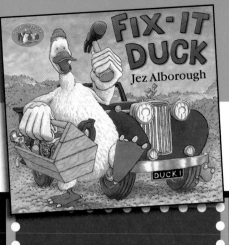

Fix-It Duck

By Jez Alborough

Is that a leak in the roof? Fix-It Duck is ready to solve the problem! One job leads to another as Duck creates havoc across the countryside with his bungled repairs.

Literacy

Duck's botched repair jobs don't affect just him; they affect his three friends too! Invite students to review all four characters with this look at story details. Give each student a paper divided into four sections. Have him draw Duck, Frog, Sheep, and Goat in separate sections. Then give a story-related clue about a character. Instruct each student to put a counter on the illustration of the corresponding character. Confirm the correct response. Continue the activity until you review a few details about each character's part in the misadventure.

Social Studies

There's no doubt about it: Duck isn't good at repairing things. What job would be a better fit for him? Help students brainstorm a list of Duck's skills. Then have each youngster write a description of a job that would be appropriate for Duck and illustrate the character at work.

Story Discussion

● Duck thinks he has bad luck. Do you agree? Explain.

● Which illustrations show that Duck is clumsy?

● What advice would you give Duck?

Writing Prompt

When Duck needs help, he turns to his friend. Write about a time you asked a friend for help.

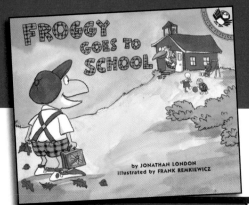

Froggy Goes to School
Written by Jonathan London and illustrated by Frank Remkiewicz

Froggy is so worried he will be late on his first day of school that he dreams he gets on the bus wearing only underwear! Fortunately, the day begins much more smoothly than Froggy imagines and leaves him in high spirits.

Literacy

When Froggy arrives at school, he is excited to see his nametag! Have each child make a nametag by writing his name on a tagboard strip and then adding an illustration of a favorite thing. When youngsters have finished their nametags, announce a child's name. Invite that child to stand and show his nametag to his classmates as he talks about his favorite thing. When he is finished, have him place his nametag in a pocket chart. Continue until each child's nametag is displayed in the pocket chart.

Math

To regain the attention of her enthusiastic students, Miss Witherspoon claps a pattern for her students to copy. Model different clapping patterns for your students to repeat. Then invite volunteers to clap patterns for their classmates to duplicate. If desired, encourage students to include snapping, stomping, or knee tapping in their patterns.

Story Discussion

- When did you realize that Froggy is dreaming at the beginning of the story?

- Froggy tells his mother he is not nervous about school. Do you believe him? Explain.

- After the principal sees Froggy modeling his swimming technique, the author describes Froggy as "looking more red in the face than green." What does the author want the reader to know?

- How do the illustrations add humor to the story? Give some examples.

Writing Prompt

List five things you think will happen on Froggy's second day of school.

Green Eggs and Ham

By Dr. Seuss

"Do you like green eggs and ham?" After a grumpy character gives a firm, negative response to this question, Sam makes a series of outlandish attempts to convince him to try the colorful cuisine.

Sam certainly offers up an unusual dinner! Invite students to imagine other strange recipes Sam might serve if he owned a restaurant. Then give each child a sheet of paper. Have him illustrate a meal that Sam might offer and then instruct him to write a caption. Bind students' papers between two covers and title the resulting book "Sam's Silly Smorgasbord."

Where do green eggs come from? While there isn't a clear answer, the possibilities can be narrowed to egg-laying animals. Draw a large egg on the board. Ask students to name various animals; then write the name of each egg-laying animal on the egg and the names of other animals outside the egg. Point out that no animals produce eggs quite like the ones Sam serves. Suggest that the eggs and ham were not green to start with. Students will surely be quick to imagine how Sam could make them green!

- Do you think the main character would be more willing to try the eggs and ham if they were not green? Why or why not?

- Do you think Sam's persistence is a good trait or a bad trait? Explain.

- What do you think the message of the story is?

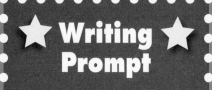

Imagine that Sam invites you to his house for green eggs and ham. Write a note telling him why you would or would not like to go.

The Grouchy Ladybug
By Eric Carle

An irritable ladybug is looking for a fight! Each hour of the day, the ill-tempered bug challenges a different animal until, with a flip of its tail, a whale reminds the bug of the importance of good manners and a positive attitude.

Speech bubbles clearly capture the exchanges between the two ladybugs. Point out to students that the speech bubbles contain only the words that the characters say. Then have each youngster draw two animals and draw and label speech bubbles to show an exchange between the critters. Display students' papers or bind them together to make a class book. Then title the collection of student work "Critter Conversations."

This hour-by-hour tale is a perfect springboard for a time-related booklet! For each student, sandwich a few white circles between two red circles and then staple them at the top. Each youngster glues a black semicircle (head) to his booklet and draws crayon details on the cover so the booklet resembles a ladybug. Next, he stamps a clockface on each page. He draws clock hands on each clock and then writes the corresponding digital time. Have more advanced students also write an appropriate activity for the time shown on each page.

★ Story Discussion ★

- Why do you think the position of the sun illustrations varies from page to page?

- Tell about a time you were exhausted at the end of the day just as the grouchy ladybug is.

- Do you think the grouchy ladybug will try to pick a fight tomorrow? Why or why not?

If you are grouchy, what can you do to get in a better mood?

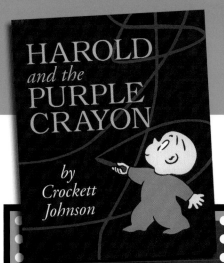

Harold and the Purple Crayon

By Crockett Johnson

A young boy creates a series of imaginative adventures with the help of a purple crayon.

Literacy

When Harold draws a purple dragon to guard his purple apple tree, he discovers that he can use his crayon to draw himself into (and out of) trouble! Revisit the illustrations from the story; then ask each child to draw a simple one-color illustration that represents a problem and its solution. For example, a child might draw himself with a very large dog and then draw a sturdy fence around the dog. Ask capable students to write captions for their illustrations. Then encourage volunteers to share their creative work with the class.

Math

A Harold-inspired math review is sure to be a hit with your youngsters. Invite each child to choose a crayon color. Then ask her to listen to your instructions. You might begin the math adventure as follows: Harold is on another nighttime adventure! This time there's a full moon in the night sky *(each child draws a circle)*. Harold decides to play a game of hopscotch, so he draws a ten-box hopscotch trail *(each child draws a trail)* and numbers the boxes from one to ten *(each child numbers her boxes)*. When he finishes playing, he's thirsty. So he draws himself 20 cents to buy himself a drink *(each child draws 20 cents)*. Then he...

Story Discussion

- Which of Harold's drawings do you think is most important? Explain.

- Do you think Harold will go on another adventure? Why?

- Would you take an adventure with Harold? Why?

- In what ways are you and Harold alike?

Writing Prompt

Use a purple crayon to draw an adventure; then write about it. Where do you go? What do you see?

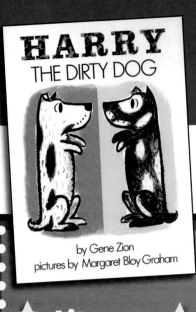

Harry the Dirty Dog

Written by Gene Zion and illustrated by Margaret Bloy Graham

Harry dislikes baths so much that he hides the scrubbing brush and runs away. He discovers that avoiding baths has a downside, though, when he returns home covered with dirt and his family doesn't recognize him!

★ Literacy ★

What causes Harry to run away? It's a tub of water! To explore this and other cause-effect relationships, draw a bathtub on a large sheet of paper. Then draw a line down the center of it to create two columns. Title the first column "Cause" and the second column "Effect." Write several cause sentences in the first column, such as "Harry plays in the coal." Next, display the poster and read each statement in turn. Have students describe its effect; then write the information in the second column.

★ Math ★

Harry's black spots seem to disappear when he gets dirty—and when students complete this subtraction activity! Make one copy of page 64. Write on the scrubbing brush a number (six or higher) from which you would like students to subtract. Place copies of the programmed page at a center along with a die and black pom-poms. A child puts the designated number of pom-poms on the dog. Then she rolls the die, removes that many pom-poms, and writes the corresponding subtraction sentence in the provided space. After she models and writes four more subtraction sentences, she colors the illustration.

★ Story Discussion ★

- In the end, Harry hides the scrubbing brush under his pillow. Why do you think he does this?

- What else could Harry have done to show his family who he is?

- What do you think will happen the next time the family tries to give Harry a bath? Why?

★ Writing Prompt ★

Write a letter to Harry encouraging him to be more cooperative at bath time. Be sure to explain why it is important to take a bath.

Hattie and the Fox
by Mem Fox
Illustrated by Patricia Mullins

Hattie and the Fox
Written by Mem Fox and illustrated by Patricia Mullins

When an unidentified animal starts to poke through nearby bushes, Hattie becomes alarmed and warns her farm friends. They disregard her increasingly specific warnings, though, until Hattie declares the animal is a fox!

 **Literacy**

This writing activity encourages students to be more attentive to descriptions than Hattie's farm friends are. Give each youngster a copy of page 65. Have him draw a secretly chosen animal in the space at the bottom right of the paper. Then ask him to describe the animal by completing the sentences. Next, instruct him to cut the dashed line to the dot and fold over the resulting flap to conceal the illustration. Pair students and have each youngster read his partner's clues, guess what the animal is, and then unfold the paper to check his guess.

 **Science**

One thing the farm animals have in common is a fear of foxes. How else do the animals compare? Display a large Venn diagram and label each circle with the name of a different animal in the story. Guide students to compare and contrast the animals; then write the information in the appropriate sections of the diagram. For more skill-stretching fun, give each youngster an individual Venn diagram and have her compare and contrast a different pair of animals.

 **Story Discussion**

- Why do you think the other animals don't seem worried about Hattie's warnings?

- What other animals fit the description Hattie gives?

- What details let you know that the story is fiction?

 **Writing Prompt**

The farm animals are so surprised in the end that none of them make a sound. Write about a time you were surprised.

If You Give a Mouse a Cookie

Written by Laura Joffe Numeroff and illustrated by Felicia Bond

What happens when a boy shares a snack with a mouse? A lot! After the mouse accepts the cookie, the little guy makes himself right at home and asks for one thing after another.

 **Literacy**

When the mouse gets what he asks for, he asks for something else! To recap the mouse's requests, give each child a copy of page 66. Ask students to color the cookie on their papers; then, as you slowly reread the story, have each child draw a line to connect the items in the order they are requested. For example, a student draws a line from the cookie to the glass of milk to the straw and so on until his line ends up back at the cookie. If time allows, invite students to complete the bonus box activity.

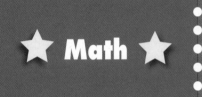 **Math**

The boy gives the mouse a chocolate chip cookie, but the mouse might have been happy with any kind of cookie! Invite youngsters to share their favorite kinds of cookies. Choose four cookies and write each name along the bottom of the board to begin making a bar graph. When the graph is ready, have each child decorate a paper circle to look like her favorite of the four cookie choices. Then invite her to tape her cookie to the graph. Add a title to the graph; then discuss the results with the group. Incorporate the words *more, fewer, most, fewest,* and *equal* as appropriate.

 **Story Discussion**

- Would you have given the mouse everything he asked for? Why or why not?

- Do you think the boy enjoyed spending time with the mouse? Explain.

- What adventures might the mouse have had if the boy had been eating a piece of fruit?

 **Writing Prompt**

The mouse and the boy had a busy day! Write about a busy day you have had.

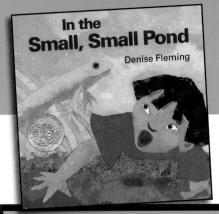

In the Small, Small Pond
By Denise Fleming

The pond is small, but it has a lot of occupants. From tadpoles that wiggle and jiggle in the spring to a frog that sleeps in the winter, a variety of critters make themselves at home in the watery world.

★ Literacy ★

The bouncy rhyming text is sure to captivate your students! After the first reading, display a large pond cutout and put lily pad cutouts nearby. As you reread the book, pause for students to identify rhyming words. Then write each rhyming word pair on a separate lily pad. Invite youngsters to attach the lily pads to the pond and use arts-and-crafts materials to add setting details. For a vocabulary-boosting extension, encourage youngsters to write sentences with the words.

★ Science ★

The agile frog takes readers from page to page and from season to season. Once students are familiar with the book, revisit the illustrations. As you encourage youngsters to notice the frog and the seasonal changes, explain that frogs hibernate in the winter. Then have each youngster visually divide a sheet of paper in half and title one half "Summer" and the other half "Winter." Have him illustrate the two halves to show what frogs do during those seasons.

★ Story ★ Discussion

- What clues does the author-illustrator use to let readers know about the change in seasons?

- Why do you think the words are arranged on the pages in different ways?

- How could you learn more about the animals and insects in the book?

★ Writing ★ Prompt

Imagine you visit the pond. Write about your visit. Be sure to describe the time of year and what you see.

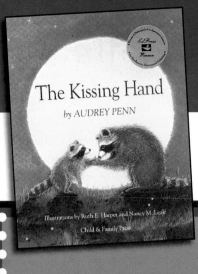

The Kissing Hand

Written by Audrey Penn and illustrated by Ruth E. Harper and Nancy M. Leak

Chester Raccoon doesn't want to leave his mother to go to school. So Chester's mother reassures him with a secret that helps him remember her love even when he is away from her.

Literacy

Your youngsters are sure to understand Chester's reluctance to try something for the first time. Invite students to talk about the first times they went someplace new, met someone new, or tried a new activity. Then ask each child to choose a personal experience to write and draw about. Instruct each child to divide a sheet of paper in half, labeling the left half "At first" and the right half "Then I." Then ask her to complete each sentence starter and illustrate her sentence to tell about a first-time experience. Encourage volunteers to share their completed projects with the group.

Science

Chester goes to school in the nighttime instead of the daytime. Ask students why they think this is and guide them to conclude that raccoons are nocturnal animals. Review the habits of nocturnal animals and then invite students to name other nocturnal animals that could be schoolmates of Chester. The book's nighttime illustrations show several possibilities!

Story Discussion

- Think about your first day at school. Did you feel similar to Chester? Explain.

- What do you think is the best way to comfort someone who is afraid?

- What did you learn about Chester when he kissed the center of his mother's hand?

Writing Prompt

The secret of the kissing hand makes Chester feel safe. Write about something that helps you feel safe when you are scared.

Lilly's Purple Plastic Purse
By Kevin Henkes

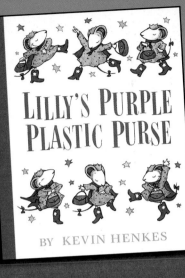

Lilly loves school and loves her teacher. However, her feelings change drastically when her teacher insists that she wait until an appropriate time to show off her brand-new purple pocketbook.

★ Literacy ★

Lilly is so wowed by her teacher that she wants to become a teacher too! Ask students what they like most about Lilly's teacher, Mr. Slinger. Explain that Mr. Slinger is a positive role model because his actions encourage positive actions in others. Next, have each child write "Wow!" at the top of a blank sheet of paper. Then ask him to illustrate and name a person he considers to be a positive role model. Invite volunteers to talk about their role models. Then encourage each child to present his work to the person he illustrated.

★ Social Studies ★

Lilly learns from her experience that it's important to keep her feelings and impulses under control. Help students identify story events in which Lilly acts with self-control and events in which she does not. Then, as a group, discuss how Lilly's actions affect her classmates. Next, show students a large lightbulb cutout. Tell them that your bright idea is to display the cutout as a reminder to practice self-discipline. Sign the cutout and invite each child to do the same!

★ Story Discussion ★

- Lilly loves everything about school. What do you love most about school?

- Do you think Mr. Slinger was right to take away Lilly's purse? Explain.

- What did you learn about Mr. Slinger when Lilly returned to school the next day?

★ Writing Prompt ★

Draw a picture of what you want to do when you grow up. Add a caption to your drawing.

The Little Red Hen
By Paul Galdone

The little red hen is tired of doing work without any help from her friends. So she puts her foot down and refuses to share even a crumb of a delicious cake she makes all by herself.

 **Literacy**

The hen's housemates change their lazy habits by the end of the story. To bring this change into full view, have each child divide a sheet of paper in half, label the left half of the paper "At the Beginning," and draw a picture that shows how the cat, dog, and mouse behave. Then have her label the right half of her paper "At the End" and draw a picture that shows how these characters change their behavior for the better.

 **Social Studies**

The cat, dog, and mouse learn an important lesson about cooperation. Ask students, "What do you think our classroom would be like if we behaved like the little red hen's friends?" After giving students time to respond, discuss the importance of cooperation and the benefits of working together. To encourage and acknowledge cooperative behaviors, softly cluck within earshot of students who are displaying the exemplary behavior.

 **Story Discussion**

- Which story character do you think you are most like? Explain.
- Do you think it is fair for the little red hen to eat all the cake? Why?
- Now that the little red hen has help around the house, what do you think she'll do with her free time?

 **Writing Prompt**

Describe ways you are helpful at home or at school.

See page 67 for a reproducible activity.

Make Way for Ducklings

By Robert McCloskey

Mr. and Mrs. Mallard find a perfect place for starting a family—a quiet area on the Charles River. After the ducklings hatch and grow, the proud mother takes them on a journey that might be dangerous without the help of a friendly police officer.

★ Literacy ★

Judging by the names of the ducklings, it seems as though Mr. and Mrs. Mallard are especially fond of words in the *-ack* word family. What if they preferred words in the *-ing* word family instead? Pose this question to students and then have them brainstorm names that end in *-ing*. Write each name on a separate blank card. Then prepare cards for one or more different rimes in the same manner. To follow up, put the cards at a center along with a pond-shaped workmat and have students sort the cards by word family.

★ Science ★

While the story about Mr. and Mrs. Mallard is fictional, careful listeners are sure to hear factual information too. To highlight several duck facts, give each youngster a copy of page 68. Read and discuss the sentences with students. Then have each student circle the word *ducks* each time it appears or ask her to circle vocabulary words. Next, instruct her to write her name on the cover and use crayons to outline the illustrations. Have her cut along the bold lines and stack the pages in order behind the cover. Then secure the stack to make a booklet.

★ Story Discussion ★

- How does Mrs. Mallard show she is a good mother?

- What are some words that describe Michael?

- Mrs. Mallard teaches the ducklings a lot. What are some things human parents teach their children?

★ Writing Prompt ★

What are three things that make a place a good home for the Mallard family? Why?

Miss Nelson Is Missing!

Written by Harry Allard and illustrated by James Marshall

Misbehaving students take their teacher, Miss Nelson, for granted until the no-nonsense Miss Viola Swamp pays them a visit.

The behavior of Miss Nelson's students changes when Miss Viola Swamp becomes their teacher. Evaluate these changes in behavior on a Venn diagram. Label one circle "Miss Nelson" and the other "Miss Swamp." Ask students to recall behaviors the students displayed for one or both teachers as you write their ideas in the appropriate sections of the diagram. Encourage students to explain why the students acted differently for the two teachers.

The two main characters of the story, Miss Nelson and Miss Swamp, have very different personalities—even though they are the same person! Discuss the unique traits of each personality and make sure students understand that the Miss Swamp disguise was worn to bring about a positive change. Next, ask students to identify possible positive changes for their classroom or school. Hopefully these changes can be made without a visit from Miss Viola Swamp!

- Is Miss Nelson a good teacher? Explain your answer.

- Do you think Miss Viola Swamp will return to Miss Nelson's classroom someday? Why?

- What did Miss Viola Swamp teach you?

- Are the kids in room 207 really keeping a secret from Miss Nelson? Why or why not?

Write a letter to your teacher. In the letter, explain why Miss Swamp will never need to visit your classroom.

Miss Rumphius
By Barbara Cooney

Alice Rumphius has three goals: to visit faraway places, to live in a home by the sea, and—the most difficult—to make the world a more beautiful place.

Literacy

Use this writing activity to inspire students to make life goals just as Alice does. Give each youngster a blank three-page booklet and have him title it "When I Grow Up." Then instruct him to title the first page "See," the second page "Do," and the third page "Live." Next, have him write and illustrate on the appropriate pages what he would like to see, what he would like to do, and where he would like to live when he is an adult. Encourage him to keep the booklet in a safe place at home so he can revisit the goals when he is older.

Social Studies

An island, the mountains, jungles, and deserts—Miss Rumphius visits a wide variety of places! Discuss with students the characteristics of each setting. Then give each child a sheet of paper divided into quarters. Have her title each section with the name of a different setting. After she adds illustrations, ask her to mark with a smiley face the setting she would most like to visit. Then have her write the reason for her choice on the back of the paper.

Story Discussion

- Why do you think Miss Rumphius likes to live by the sea?

- Miss Rumphius wants to do three things. Which one is the biggest challenge? Why?

- Why do you think some people call Miss Rumphius "That Crazy Old Lady"?

Writing Prompt

Imagine you are Miss Rumphius visiting a faraway place. Write a letter to a friend telling about your trip.

The Mitten

The Mitten

By Jan Brett

When Nicki goes outdoors to play, he unknowingly drops one of his mittens in the snow. Several woodland creatures find shelter in the cozy mitten until a bear's sneeze disrupts their rest.

Literacy

From the mole tunneling along to the bear lumbering by, each animal makes his entrance into the story in a different way. After a first reading, revisit each page where an animal comes onto the scene and enters the mitten. Clarify any vocabulary that is unfamiliar to students. Then assign each student a different animal. (Assign more than one student to the same animal if necessary.) As you reread the story, encourage each student to pantomime his assigned animal's actions. It's a kid-pleasing way to build vocabulary!

Math

All the animals except the mouse enter the mitten in a very orderly way: by size! Guide students to notice this detail. Then display several number cards in random order. (For best results, do not display all the numbers from a counting sequence.) Next, show students a large mitten. Have them put the number cards in the mitten, one at a time, from the smallest to the largest number. Repeat the activity with different cards for more number order reinforcement.

Story Discussion

- Do you think Nicki has lost mittens in the past? Explain.
- Why does the mole let the rabbit in the mitten? Why do the rabbit and mole let the hedgehog in the mitten?
- Do you think Nicki will wear the mittens again? Why or why not?

Writing Prompt

In the end, Baba notices that one mitten is bigger than the other. How might Nicki explain the size difference?

Officer Buckle and Gloria
By Peggy Rathmann

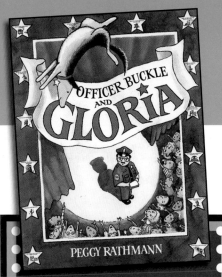

No one at Napville School listens to Officer Buckle's presentations before he teams up with a crowd-pleasing canine named Gloria. The dog's popularity makes Officer Buckle feel he's not needed—that is, until the school has its biggest accident ever!

★ Literacy ★

What a difference a buddy can make! Review with students how successful the safety presentations are when Officer Buckle and Gloria team up. Then have each youngster cut out a colorful copy of the star pattern from page 69. Instruct him to label one side "With a Buddy" and the other side "Without a Buddy." Ask him to write or draw corresponding story details on each side. Suspend students' stars for a bright reminder of the story's message about friends and teamwork.

★ Social Studies ★

The Napville staff and students learn the hard way that inattention to rules can have disastrous consequences. To help your students keep important rules top of mind, divide them into groups. Have each group create a poster for an assigned category of safety tips, such as classroom rules, playground rules, and fire safety. Invite the group members to decorate the posters with star illustrations or stickers. Then ask them to present their tips to the class. Officer Buckle would be proud!

★ Story Discussion ★

- Why is it important to follow safety rules?

- Why do you think there are no accidents when Officer Buckle does the presentations with Gloria?

- How would you feel if you were Officer Buckle and Gloria got all the attention? Explain.

★ Writing Prompt ★

Write a letter inviting Officer Buckle and Gloria to your school. Be sure to tell why they should come.

Olivia
By Ian Falconer

Olivia is a precocious piglet with boundless energy. She builds a sand castle skyscraper, paints a modern masterpiece, and challenges everyone to keep up with her.

Literacy

It's easy to understand why Olivia exhausts her mother—she's always on the go. Use Olivia's actions to publish a student-friendly writing reference. Ask students to recall actions that Olivia performs during the story as you write their ideas on the board. When you have one action per student, give each child a sheet of paper on which to copy and illustrate a different action from the list. Bind the papers between two red construction paper covers and title the volume "Olivia's Action Words."

Science

Olivia is always busy—no matter what the weather! Give each child a copy of page 70. Have students recall what Olivia does in sunny weather and then ask each child to illustrate the summer section of her paper accordingly. In a similar manner, invite each child to illustrate each remaining section of her paper with a weather-appropriate activity she thinks Olivia might enjoy.

Story Discussion

● How can you tell Olivia has a great imagination?

● Why do you think Olivia's little brother, Ian, copies her?

● Would you like to spend a day with Olivia? Explain.

Writing Prompt

Olivia likes to do many things. List some things that you like to do.

The Pigeon Finds a Hot Dog!

By Mo Willems

A clever duckling tries to persuade a pigeon to give up the hot dog he's found, but the pigeon isn't falling for the duckling's antics. In the end, a compromise is made and the twosome share the delicious hot dog.

★ Literacy ★

This story, written as a dialogue between a pigeon and a duckling, provides the perfect opportunity to investigate speech bubbles. In the center of a large sheet of bulletin board paper, draw a simple pigeon with a speech bubble that contains the words "Ooooh! A hot dog!" Have each child draw a self-portrait on her paper. Next, have her draw a speech bubble and program it with a reply. Invite volunteers to share their pictures and words before you post the projects with the pigeon.

★ Math ★

At the end of the story, the pigeon finally agrees to share his hot dog with the duckling. For a review of equal and unequal parts, have each child draw two hot dogs on her paper. Ask her to divide one hot dog into equal parts and the other into unequal parts. Then have her label her illustrations "Equal" and "Unequal" accordingly.

★ Story Discussion ★

- Do you think the duckling is being truthful when he says he's never had a hot dog before? Why?

- Why do you think the pigeon agrees to share the hot dog?

- Why is the text in the book different sizes?

★ Writing Prompt ★

In the center of a sheet of paper, draw your favorite food. Around your drawing, write words or phrases describing how the food tastes.

Polar Bear, Polar Bear, What Do You Hear?

Written by Bill Martin Jr. and illustrated by Eric Carle

A trip to the zoo introduces young readers to a multitude of animals and the sounds they make.

Literacy

Each zoo animal in this delightful tale makes a unique sound. Write each sound-related verb on a separate card and ask volunteers to illustrate the animals on individual cards. Display each verb card with its matching animal illustration. As students practice making each animal sound, show them the corresponding verb and picture cards. Then, with a neighboring class or two in attendance, read the book aloud. Pause after each sound-related verb and wait while students interject the appropriate animal sound. Keep the verb and animal cards on display and encourage students to incorporate the verbs in future writing assignments.

Literacy

How important is the setting of this story? Very important indeed! Ask students how the story would change if the setting were a farm, a circus, or another location. Next, give each child two or three copies of the booklet pages on page 71 so she can write and illustrate her ideas! To make a booklet, have each child cut out her booklet pages, staple them in order between two construction paper covers, and then add a title and illustration to the front cover. Who is ready to read?

Story Discussion

- Which animals from the story have you seen in person?

- What would be the best or worst part about being a zookeeper?

- Would you rather go to a zoo or a circus? Explain.

Writing Prompt

Make a list of sounds you might hear on a farm, at a circus, or near a pond.

The Rainbow Fish

By Marcus Pfister

The Rainbow Fish is dazzling, but he's also proud, selfish, and unhappy. It's not until he follows the sage advice of the octopus that he discovers true happiness.

Literacy

What the most beautiful fish in the ocean learns about friendship is at the heart of the story—and this class activity! Post a large fish cutout. Cut from colorful paper two scales per student. Have students write an act of kindness on each of their scales or dictate the information for you to write. Attach the scales to the fish. Then share your ideas for showing kindness as you add a few foil scales to the fish. Post the title "Get in the Swim of Kindness!" to complete the community-building display.

Math

Rainbow Fish discovers that subtracting scales is fun. Your students are sure to agree with this story problem follow-up. Have each youngster color a copy of page 72 and cut out the scales. Then describe relevant subtraction problems, such as "The fish has six scales. It gives away two scales. How many scales does it have left?" Ask students to model and solve the problems. If desired, also have each student write the corresponding subtraction sentences on a separate page.

Story Discussion

- What happens when Rainbow Fish is selfish? Explain.

- What do you think would have happened if Rainbow Fish shared his scales the first time the little blue fish asked?

- How does sharing make Rainbow Fish feel? How do you feel when someone shares with you?

Writing Prompt

Rainbow Fish is happy when he shares with his friends. List things that make you happy.

Russell the Sheep

By Rob Scotton

Russell the sheep is a sheep that can't sleep! Tag along with Russell as he tries with all his might to fall into a restful slumber.

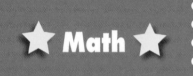
★ Literacy ★

Russell tries many different ways to fall asleep. Ask each child to include her favorites of Russell's attempts in a booklet. First, have each child cut out the booklet backing and pages from a copy of page 73. Help her stack the pages atop the backing and staple the pages in place. Then, on each booklet page and the backing, invite each child to draw a picture of one way Russell tries to fall asleep. Encourage students to use their booklets to retell the story.

★ Math ★

Maybe if Russell had skip-counted sheep, he could have fallen asleep faster! Use cotton balls (sheep) to lead students in counting by ones. Then guide the class in counting sheep by twos, fives, and tens. For an independent follow-up activity, give each child a handful of cotton balls (sheep) and a paper strip. Have him arrange the sheep on the strip in groups of two or five, glue them in place, and then program the strip for skip-counting.

★ Story Discussion ★

- What suggestions would you give Russell to help him fall asleep?

- How does the book's author add humor to the story? Explain.

- When do you think Russell will wake up? Why?

- How do you think Russell will feel when he wakes up?

★ Writing Prompt ★

Write five reasons why it is important to get a good night's sleep.

The Seasons of Arnold's Apple Tree

By Gail Gibbons

Throughout the year, a young boy enjoys his secret place and the apple tree that grows there.

 **Literacy**

There's no doubt Arnold's activities will remind students of their own pastimes. To explore students' text-to-self connections, have each youngster visually divide a sheet of paper in half. Instruct her to write on one half "In the [season], Arnold [verb phrase]." Ask her to write a similar sentence on the other half of the paper telling about an activity she does during the same season. Then encourage her to illustrate her work. Showcase students' work in groups by season and title the display "Seasonal Connections."

 **Science**

One thing that makes Arnold's tree special is that it changes along with the seasons. Discuss with students how the tree looks at different times of the year. Then give each child a copy of page 74. Guide him to label each page with the appropriate season. Then ask him to color the pages, cut them out, and stack them in order, beginning with spring. After you staple the stack between two paper rectangles, have the youngster title the booklet. It's a great tool for retelling the story!

 **Story Discussion**

- What do you think a perfect secret place would be like?
- How do Arnold's clothes reflect seasonal changes?
- It's spring at the end of the story. What might Arnold do?

 **Writing Prompt**

Apples taste great plain and in recipes. Write how to make your favorite apple snack.

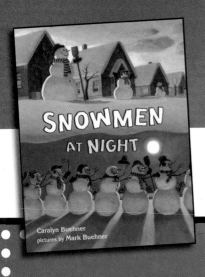

Snowmen at Night

Written by Caralyn Buehner and illustrated by Mark Buehner

One wintry day, a young child builds a glorious snowman. But the following morning, his snowman is droopy and disheveled—which leads him to imagine what snowmen really do at night!

 **Literacy**

No snow is needed to build this snowman; however, an ear for rhyming words comes in very handy! Reread the story and pause after reading aloud each grouping of text. Invite a volunteer to name any rhyming words he hears. When a youngster identifies a pair of rhyming words, he draws one part of a snowman on the board. If, at the end of the story, the snowman drawing needs a few more details, invite volunteers to name more rhyming word pairs.

Science

The snowmen in the story have a great time playing at night. To help students compare the conditions of daytime play to nighttime play, ask questions that include the following: What happens to the sun at night? What happens to the temperature at night? Would it make a difference if the nighttime sky was cloudy or clear? Also pose play-related questions, such as "What games could you play at night?" and "Would you need any special equipment?" Then ask each child to draw or write his nighttime play ideas on a copy of page 75. Encourage interested students to develop their ideas into stories.

 **Story Discussion**

- Is this story real or make-believe? How do you know?
- Why do you think the snowmen only play at night?
- Which activity would you enjoy doing with the snowmen the most? Why?
- Why do you think the snowmen in this story drink ice-cold cocoa instead of hot cocoa?

 **Writing Prompt**

Write a make-believe story about another object that plays at night.

Strega Nona

By Tomie dePaola

When Big Anthony disregards Strega Nona's directions and uses her magic pasta pot, he accidentally causes a large pasta problem! Fortunately, Strega Nona returns just in time to save everyone from harm.

★ Literacy ★

Big Anthony tries shouting at the pot, lifting it, and sitting on top of it to stop the flood of pasta. Ask students what pasta-stopping tactics they might try if they were faced with the pasta problem. Welcome a variety of suggestions; then ask each child to draw or write a solution on paper. Bind the students' work between construction paper covers and add the title "Pasta-Pot Solutions." Place the class book in your classroom library or reading center.

★ Math ★

How much pasta can a pasta pot hold? Strega Nona knows. Do your students? Ask each child to draw a pasta pot on her paper. Then give her an uncooked pasta shape, such as a butterfly, cartwheel, or twist. (If pasta is not an option, use Unifix cubes or another manipulative.) First, ask her to write an estimate on her paper of how many pasta shapes are needed to cover her pot. Next, have her use a supply of pasta to check her estimate. Instruct each child to compare her pasta count to her estimate; then invite her to share her results with the class.

★ Story Discussion ★

● Do you think Strega Nona regrets hiring Big Anthony? Why?

● What do you think Big Anthony learns from his pasta experience?

● How would the story have been different if the magic pot were filled with soup instead of pasta?

● Why does Strega Nona want Big Anthony's punishment to fit his crime?

★ Writing Prompt ★

Pretend you are Big Anthony. Write a letter to Strega Nona apologizing for your actions.

See page 76 for a reproducible activity.

Swimmy

By Leo Lionni

A tiny fish comes up with an ingenious plan to keep a school of little red fish safe. What's the key to the plan? It's teamwork!

 **Literacy**

The descriptions of the marvels Swimmy observes are sure to inspire your young writers! After students are familiar with the story, reread the descriptions. Discuss how the author uses figurative language to create word pictures. Then ask each youngster to draw an ocean animal and write a descriptive caption with the format "Swimmy sees [a sea urchin] as [pointy] as [a pin cushion]."

Social Studies

When the tiny fish work together, they have a huge achievement! Have students brainstorm ways they can work together to make the school a better place. Write each idea on a separate sentence strip. To showcase the ideas, have each youngster write his name or initials on a small red fish cutout. Arrange the fish on a bulletin board to form one large fish shape. Add a small black fish for an eye. Then display the sentence strips around the fish and add the title "A Great School Begins With Teamwork!"

 **Story Discussion**

- Why do you think Swimmy is the only fish in his school that escapes from the tuna?

- What makes Swimmy happy?

- How would you describe Swimmy? Why?

 **Writing Prompt**

Write about a time you worked with others to accomplish something.

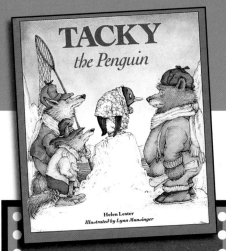

Tacky the Penguin

By Helen Lester

All the penguins know that Tacky is odd. What the bird buddies are about to learn is that an odd bird can be a great bird to have around!

Tacky is a one-of-a-kind penguin! Invite students to comment on how Tacky is different from his companions. List students' observations on a large Venn diagram that resembles two over-lapped icebergs. Then review the lists. Guide students to understand that Tacky's unusual appearance and behavior causes no problems and ultimately helps him and his companions survive. What a great reminder that individual differences are grand!

Even though Tacky's story is fiction, you can use his tale to reinforce penguin facts! During a rereading of the story, challenge youngsters to identify penguin truths. *(Penguins live in a cold climate; can swim, dive, and stand upright; and are black and white.)* Use a copy of the booklet activity on page 77 for additional reinforcement. To make a booklet, a student cuts out the cover and pages. He stacks the pages in order behind the cover and staples the left margin; then he illustrates each page.

- What do the penguin names Goodly, Lovely, Angel, Neatly, and Perfect tell you about the individual penguins? What about the name Tacky?

- Why do you think Tacky greets the hunters instead of hiding from them?

- In what ways are you like Tacky?

Tacky is a unique and special penguin. Write about things that make you a unique and special person!

Tops & Bottoms

By Janet Stevens

Lazy Bear discovers it's a mistake to go into a planting and harvesting business with a neighbor, especially when the neighbor is as clever as Hare.

Literacy

Bear and Hare seem as different as two business partners can be. Bear is lazy and rich. Hare is hardworking and poor. However, the two neighbors do have a few things in common. Draw a large Venn diagram on the board, labeling one side "Bear" and the other side "Hare." Invite students to compare and contrast the characters as you list students' responses on the diagram.

Science

The plan Hare cooks up with his wife to feed their family works! Instruct each child to position a blank sheet of paper horizontally and then draw two vertical lines to make three equal-size columns. Have him label the columns, from left to right, "Bottom," "Top," and "Middle." Next, have each child color and cut out the cards from a copy of page 78, sort the story cards on his paper according to Hare's terminology, and glue them in place. Invite students to use their papers to retell the story of Bear and Hare. To extend the learning, help students categorize each of the three extra vegetables as a bottom, top, or middle before they incorporate the cards into their sorts.

Story Discussion

● Bear thinks Hare cheats him out of the best parts of the crops. What do you think?

● What does Bear learn from Hare? How does he change his ways?

● Do you think Bear will be tricked again by Hare? Explain.

Writing Prompt

Pretend you are Bear. Write a letter to Hare thanking him for helping you change your ways.

The Very Hungry Caterpillar

By Eric Carle

Each day for a week, a growing caterpillar eats increasingly larger amounts of food. He then retreats into a cocoon to rest (and to recover from a very full belly) before he emerges as a beautiful butterfly!

Literacy

The daily sequence of the caterpillar's story provides the perfect structure for retelling practice. Give each child a copy of page 79 to complete. When she finishes, the caterpillar's daily diet will be pictured. Then have her practice retelling the story with a partner, using her paper to guide her.

Science

The caterpillar's weeklong eating spree invites a review of the five food groups. Recall that on Monday through Friday the hungry caterpillar munches only on fruit. Then ask the youngsters to name foods the caterpillar could eat if he ate only from one of the other food groups (milk and dairy; grains; vegetables; meat, beans, fish, and nuts). Next, give each child a card on which to draw and label one of the foods mentioned. With your students' help, read a milk and dairy version of the story, a grains version of the story, and so on. Perhaps a "well-balanced" story version is in order too!

Story Discussion

● Why do you think the caterpillar gets a stomachache?

● What parts of the story could really happen?

● What parts of the story could not really happen?

● What do you think the butterfly will do first? Why?

Writing Prompt

Make a grocery list of the foods from the story that you like to eat.

Waiting for Wings Lois Ehlert

Waiting for Wings

By Lois Ehlert

Caterpillars hatch from eggs and begin their journey to becoming butterflies. The vivid spring garden illustrations and rhyming text cheerfully teach little ones about the life cycle of a butterfly.

Literacy

Cling, grow, hatch, and fly! The characters in this book sure are busy! On the board, draw a simple butterfly outline. Reread the story, asking students to listen for action words. Each time an action word is identified, write it on the butterfly outline. For an added challenge, ask each child to choose a word from the board and use it in a sentence. Have him write the sentence on a sheet of paper and add an illustration.

Science

Discussing the sequence of this story doubles as a way to teach the life cycle of a butterfly! Have each child color and cut out a copy of the booklet pages on page 80. Have him order the pages to match the story's sequence and then help him staple his booklet together along the left side. Each time a student reads his booklet, he reviews the story sequence and the life cycle of a butterfly.

Story Discussion

- What facts did you learn about butterflies?

- How does the author use illustrations to help tell the story?

- When the author writes "We've been waiting for wings!" what creature is saying this? How do you know?

Writing Prompt

Draw and color a butterfly. Write a description of your butterfly.

Where the Wild Things Are

By Maurice Sendak

After Max is sent to bed for his mischievous behavior, he imagines traveling far away to where the wild things are.

Literacy

The combination of real and fantastic story details is sure to captivate young listeners! To distinguish the details, make a two-column chart. Draw Max's supper bowl at the top of one column and label it "Real." Draw a crown at the top of the other column and label it "Fantasy." Post the chart after students are familiar with the story. Then, with student input, write story details in the appropriate columns of the chart. Review the information in each column to clarify what really happens the night Max wears his wolf suit.

Science

What if a sailboat didn't appear? What else could Max have used to float across the ocean? After students brainstorm a list of potential items, set out a shallow container of water and several items whose buoyancy students can test. Then have youngsters predict and determine which items float. It's sure to spark ideas for seaworthy alternatives for Max!

Story Discussion

- What is a wild rumpus?

- Why does Max leave the place where the wild things are?

- Why do you think Max's mother takes his supper to him even though he was sent to his room?

Writing Prompt

What do you think happens next? Explain.

The Wolf's Chicken Stew

By Keiko Kasza

When a greedy wolf decides to fatten up a chicken for dinner, the plan he cooks up takes a surprising twist.

★ Literacy ★

Mr. Wolf's craving for chicken stew sends him in search of a delicious chicken. Ask students what it means to crave something. Invite them to describe food cravings they have and how these cravings make them feel. Then give your vocabulary discussion an interesting twist by asking students to suggest how the wolf's tale might have been told if, instead of craving a delicious chicken stew, he craved a pepperoni pizza! Help students identify a beginning, a middle, and an end to their scrumptious story.

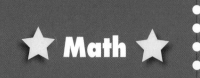
★ Math ★

One hundred pancakes, 100 doughnuts, a 100-pound cake, and 100 cookies—all prepared by the wolf—clearly invite a counting-to-100 activity! Have students sit in a circle. Distribute 100 round counters (cookies) and provide a cookie sheet with raised edges. For a counting-by-ones activity, have each child, in turn, place his cookies one by one on the cookie sheet as the group counts. For skip-counting, have students work together to form stacks of five (or ten) cookies each. Then, one by one, have students place the cookie stacks on the cookie sheet as the group skip-counts to 100.

★ Story Discussion

- What details from the story suggest that the wolf likes to bake?

- Why do you think the wolf delivers his baked goods only at night?

- Do you think the chicken knew who was bringing the treats? Explain.

- Would you like to be friends with the wolf and the chicken? Explain.

★ Writing Prompt ★

List things you would like the wolf to bring to you.

Name _____

• • • • • • • • • • **Watch It Grow!** • • • • • • • • •

 Cut. Glue in order.

✏ Write.

1	_____

	_____

2	_____

	_____

3	_____

	_____

4	_____

	_____

Read-Aloud Roundup • ©The Mailbox® Books • TEC61316

Note to the teacher: Use with the literacy activity on page 7.

· · · · · · · · · · Looks Yummy! · · · · · · · · ·

Use the code.

 Draw.

 Color the to match.

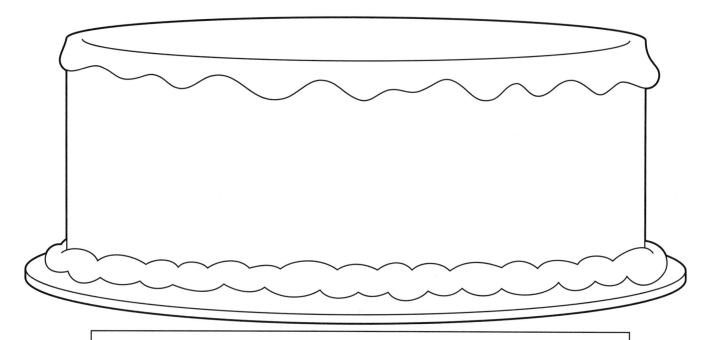

Code

☆—1¢   ♡—1¢   ✿—1¢   🕯—2¢

Read-Aloud Roundup • ©The Mailbox® Books • TEC61316

56   **Note to the teacher:** Use with the math activity on page 10.

Name _____

Bunny Baker

Count.

Color to make a graph.

Cake Decorations

	1	2	3	4	5	6	7	8
☆ star								
🌹 rose								
♡ heart								
🕯 candle								

Write how many.

 _____

 _____

 _____

 _____

Circle.

Which has the **most**?

Which has the **fewest**?

Name _____

58

Beautiful Blooms

chrysanthemum

delphinium

Cut.

Glue.

Read-Aloud Roundup • ©The Mailbox® Books • TEC61316

flower	flower	stem	stem	roots	leaf	leaf

Note to the teacher: Use with the science activity on page 12.

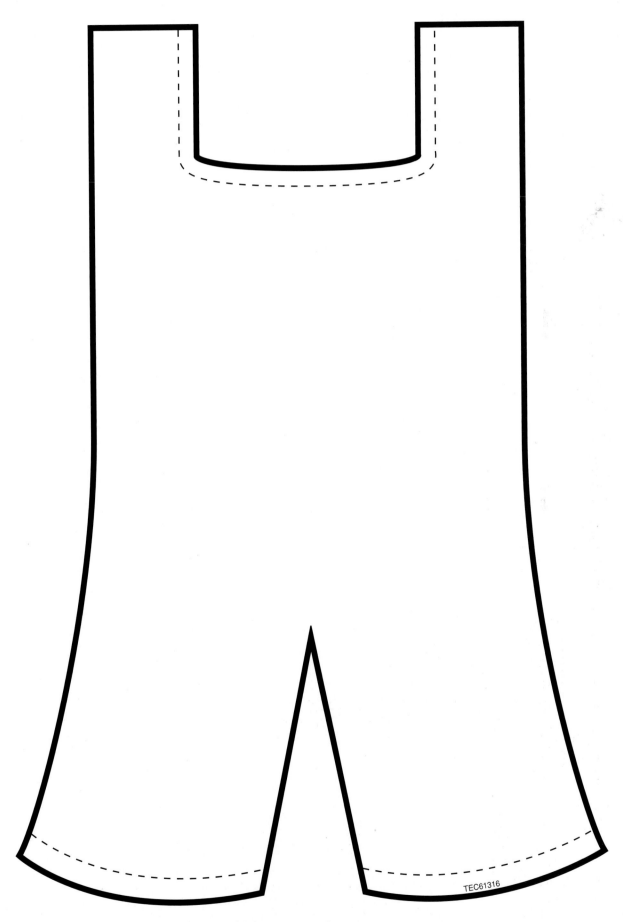

TEC61316

I can share my things.

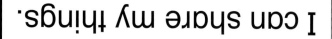

I can share my snack.

I can share my time.

I can share

Name _____

Read-Aloud Roundup • ©The Mailbox® Books • TEC61316

Note to the teacher: Use with the literacy idea on page 19. Cut along the bold line on a copy of this page. Fold along the thin horizontal line (keeping the programming to the outside) and then fold along the thin vertical line (keeping the cover to the outside).

• • • • • • • • • • • • • • **Door Pattern** • • • • • • • • **Pet Cards**

Use with the literacy activity on page 20.   Use with the math activity on page 20.

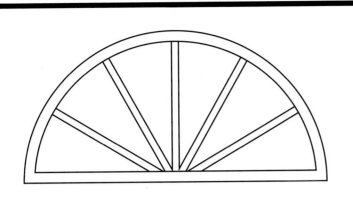

Knock!

Knock!

Knock!

It is a...

TEC61316

Elephant Cards •

Use with the math activity on page 21.

TEC61316

TEC61316

TEC61316

TEC61316

TEC61316

TEC61316

Read-Aloud Roundup • ©The Mailbox® Books • TEC61316

Name _____

Fishy Lineups

Read.

Count.

Color.

four purple fish

three orange fish

six striped fish

two spotted fish

five green-and-yellow striped fish

Note to the teacher: Use with the second literacy activity on page 22.

• • • • • • • Disappearing Spots • • • • • • •

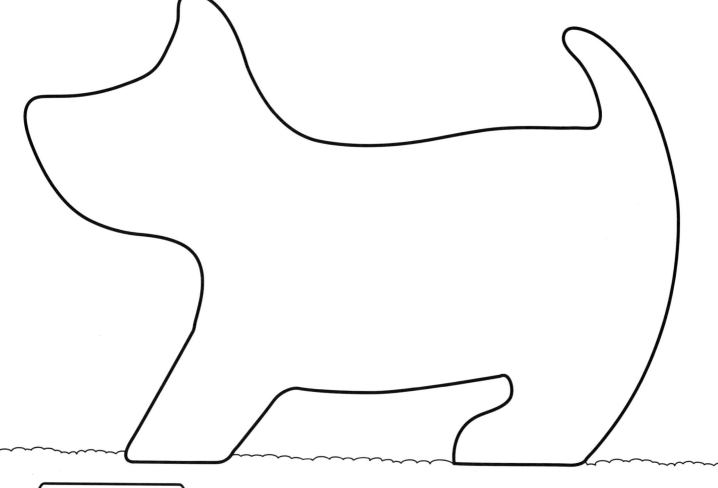

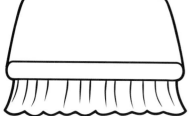

A. _____ – _____ = _____

B. _____ – _____ = _____

C. _____ – _____ = _____

D. _____ – _____ = _____

E. _____ – _____ = _____

Read-Aloud Roundup • ©The Mailbox® Books • TEC61316

64   **Note to the teacher:** Use with the math activity on page 28.

· · · · · · · · · **Mystery Animal** · · · · · · · · · ·

 Draw.  Write.

✂ Cut.

Fold.

1. I see _____ eyes.

2. I see _____ ears.

3. I see _____ legs.

4. I see _____ on its body.

5. I hear _____.

What is it?

 Draw here.

Fold.

Note to the teacher: Use with the first literacy activity on page 29.

Name _____

. . . . One Thing Leads to Another . . . .

Listen.

Bonus: On the back of this paper, draw what you think happens next.

Read-Aloud Roundup • ©The Mailbox® Books • TEC61316

66   **Note to the teacher:** Use with the literacy idea on page 30.

Name _____

Freshly Baked Bread

✂ Cut. 🖊 Glue in order.

1	2	3	4

✏ Write.

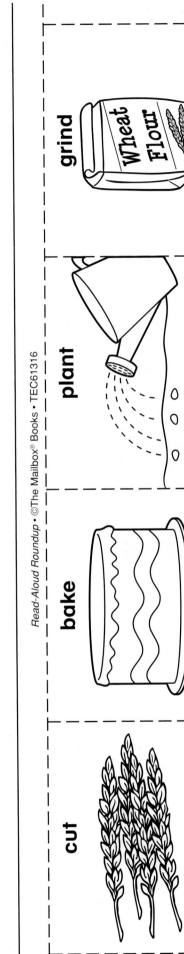

grind

plant

bake

cut

Read-Aloud Roundup • ©The Mailbox® Books • TEC61316

Note to the teacher: Use with *"The Little Red Hen"* on page 34.

67

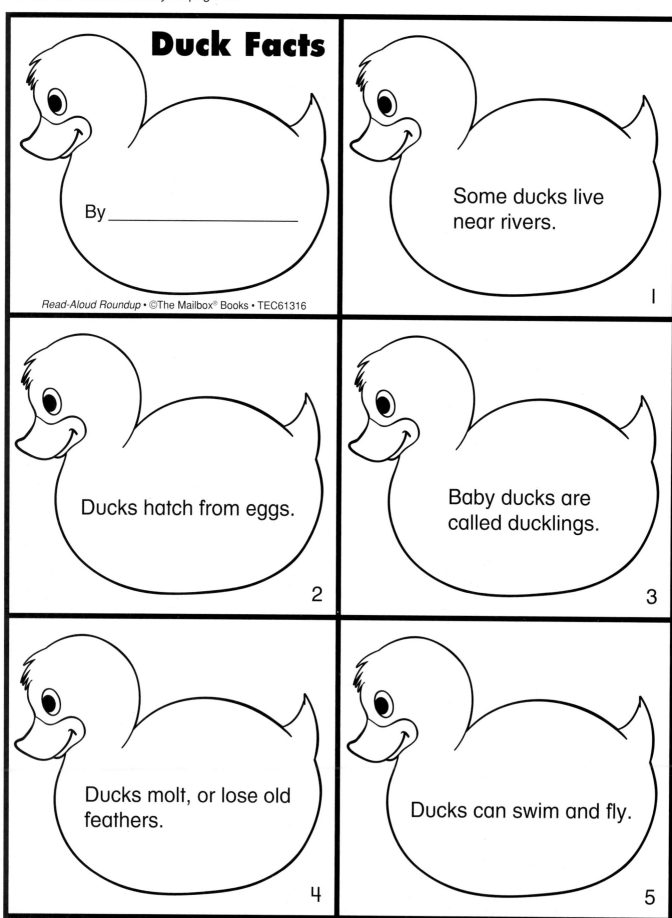

Duck Facts

By _____

Read-Aloud Roundup • ©The Mailbox® Books • TEC61316

Some ducks live near rivers.

1

Ducks hatch from eggs.

2

Baby ducks are called ducklings.

3

Ducks molt, or lose old feathers.

4

Ducks can swim and fly.

5

TEC61316

• • • • • • • • • • • • **A Busy Pig** • • • • • • • • • •

 **Fall**

 **Winter**

 **Spring**

 **Summer**

Note to the teacher: Use with the science idea on page 40.

What do you hear?

I hear a _____ in my ear.

Read-Aloud Roundup • ©The Mailbox® Books • TEC61316

What do you hear?

I hear a _____ in my ear.

Read-Aloud Roundup • ©The Mailbox® Books • TEC61316

• • • • • • • • • **Scale Subtraction** • • • • • • • •

Listen for directions.

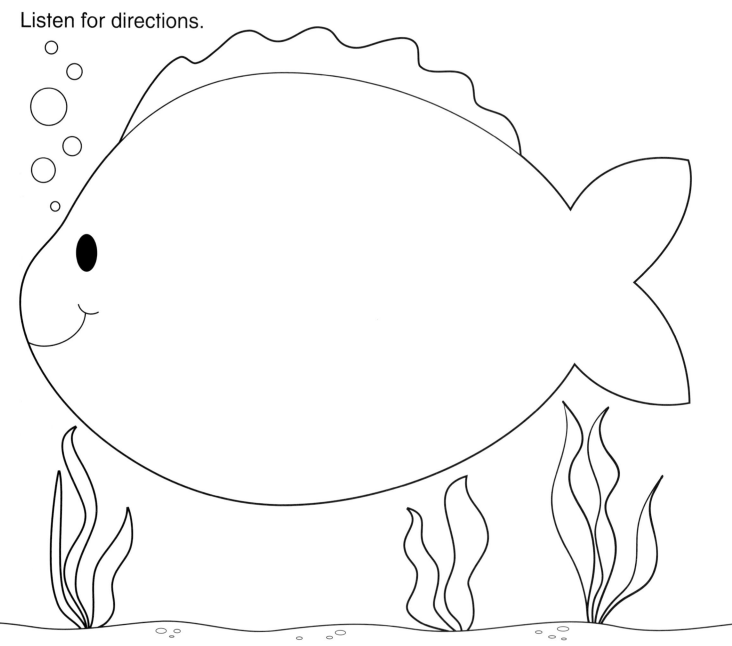

Read-Aloud Roundup • ©The Mailbox® Books • TEC61316

TEC61316 TEC61316 TEC61316 TEC61316 TEC61316

TEC61316 TEC61316 TEC61316 TEC61316 TEC61316

Note to the teacher: Use with the math activity on page 43.

Read-Aloud Roundup • ©The Mailbox® Books • TEC61316

Booklet Pages

Use with the science activity on page 45.

Read-Aloud Roundup • ©The Mailbox® Books • TEC61316

Name

Nighttime Play

Where will you play?

What games will you play?

Which night?

Who will be there?

Read-Aloud Roundup • ©The Mailbox® Books • TEC61316

Note to the teacher: Use with the science activity on page 46.

What's Cookin'?

Write.

Draw.

Bubble, bubble, _____ pot.

Cook me some _____, nice and hot.

I am hungry. I want a treat.

Cook some _____ for me to eat.

Thank you, thank you, my _____ pot.

I have my _____, nice and hot.

Please cool off; stop the heat.

I have lots of food to eat.

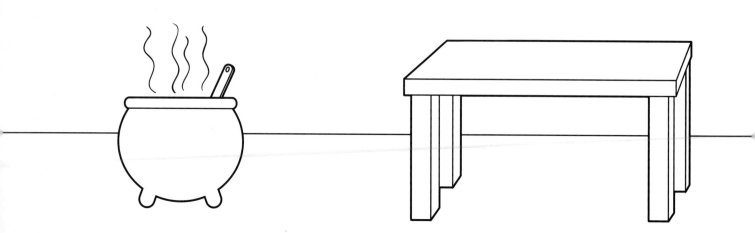

Note to the teacher: Use with *"Strega Nona"* on page 47. Have each child choose a favorite cooked food and write its name in each blank. Then have each child finish the picture by adding a self-likeness, the favorite food, and other desired details.

A Very Cool Bird!

Read-Aloud Roundup • ©The Mailbox® Books • TEC61316

It swims fast.

1

It dives deep.

2

It waddles to and fro.

3

It does a super belly slide

4

Upon the ice and snow.

5

Use with the science activity on page 50.

corn

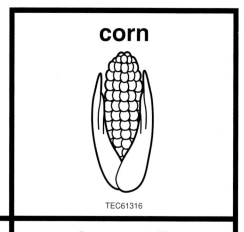

TEC61316

carrot

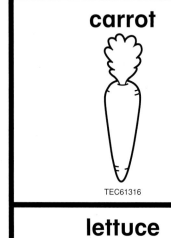

TEC61316

celery

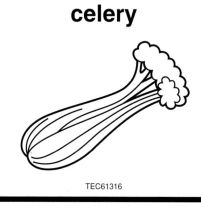

TEC61316

broccoli

TEC61316

lettuce

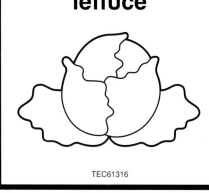

TEC61316

beet

TEC61316

radish

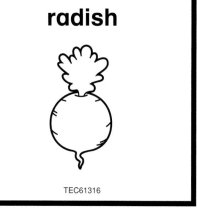

TEC61316

extra cards

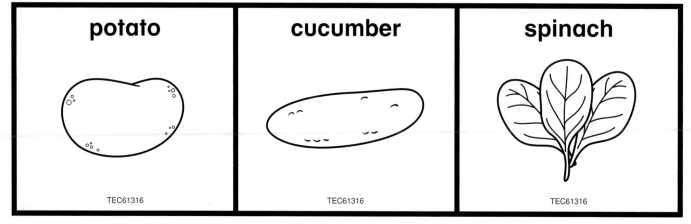

potato

TEC61316

cucumber

TEC61316

spinach

TEC61316

Read-Aloud Roundup • ©The Mailbox® Books • TEC61316

Name _____

A Caterpillar's Story

✏️ Draw.

Monday	Tuesday	Wednesday	Thursday

Friday	Saturday	Sunday
	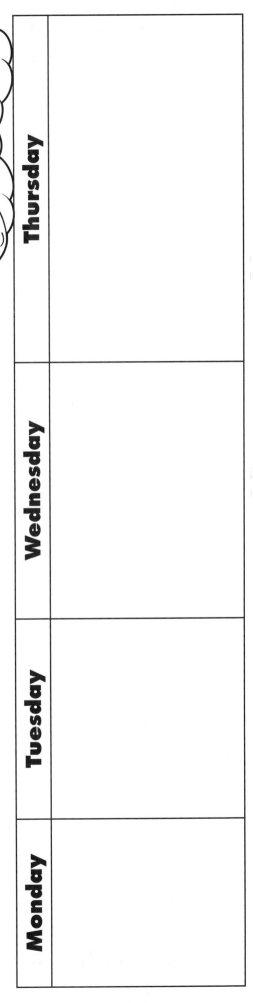	

Note to the teacher: Use with the literacy idea on page 51.

Booklet Pages

Use with the science idea on page 52.

Eggs are laid.

1

They fly away.

(Go to page 1.)

Read-Aloud Roundup • ©The Mailbox® Books • TEC61316

6

Caterpillars hatch.
They eat.

2

They sip nectar.

5

They find a place to sleep.

3

When it is time, butterflies
are born.

4